IMAGES
of England

SADDLEWORTH

A rainy day in Dobcross Square for the Whitsuntide Festival in 1914.

IMAGES
of England

SADDLEWORTH

Compiled by
Michael Fox and Peter Fox

TEMPUS

First published 2001
Copyright © Michael Fox and Peter Fox, 2001

Tempus Publishing Limited
The Mill, Brimscombe Port,
Stroud, Gloucestershire, GL5 2QG

ISBN 0 7524 2275 8

Typesetting and origination by
Tempus Publishing Limited
Printed in Great Britain by
Midway Colour Print, Wiltshire

Church-fields, *c.* 1910. A local teacher stands with a group of pupils for an informal portrait. The house behind was known lcoally as 'the house with knobs on'! A local paper in 1962 described this building as a 'blemish on the fair face of the village'. Its loss is now lamented.

Contents

Major Collins, the Commanding Officer of the Volunteers' Encampment, Uppermill, 1879.

Introduction

The photographs in this album provide a window into the past of a vibrant community in the Pennine borderland between Lancashire and Yorkshire. Although much has been written about Saddleworth, arguably it is the photographic image that is the most powerful in giving a sense of what this diverse area of valley-bottom villages, hillside hamlets, textile mills and varied traditions was really like.

The majority of the photographs date from the early 1900s. It is ironic in an age when technology has made it easier and cheaper to record images than ever before that photographs of Saddleworth taken a century ago seem far more plentiful than those of modern origin. For this we have the commercial postcard to thank, the huge popularity of which at the beginning of the twentieth century created a demand for photographs of everyday scenes and events that nowadays are recorded only haphazardly, if at all.

The authors hope that this publication will encourage photographers of the present day to record Saddleworth as it is now for the benefit of historians in the future. This would be a fitting tribute to those early photographers without whose skill and vision this book would not have been possible.

Peter and Michael Fox
October 2001

Acknowledgements

The authors owe a great debt to the many individuals who over the years have lent old photographs of Saddleworth. Numerous thanks are also due to those who have not only researched the history of the district so thoroughly but have made their work freely available for the enjoyment of others.

One
Villages

Diggle from Harrop Edge, c. 1900. Running from right to left through the photograph is Huddersfield Road. It was the building of housing along this former turnpike road of 1796 that gradually changed Diggle from a group of isolated hamlets into a village. This location was also shaped by the canal and main-line railway that converged here in the first half of the nineteenth century, both of which can be seen at the top. Tips of the spoil removed from the railway tunnels under the Standedge ridge to Marsden flank the late eighteenth-century Wharf Mill in the centre.

Denshaw from Brownhill Naze, *c.* 1900. This part of the village was once known as 'Junction' because of the several turnpike roads that converged here. Sweeping down the hillside is one of these, the Oldham – Ripponden road, which opened in 1798. Among the buildings at the sides of this road is a terrace of five cottages, Wibsey, at which the Denshaw Co-operative Society was formed in 1857.

Denshaw crossroads. The motor vehicles parked by the road to Delph place this view in the 1920s. The tower belongs to Christ Church. This was built in the 1860s by Henry Gartside, a solicitor who lived in Greenfield and was to become the first town clerk of Ashton-under-Lyne.

Denshaw from Woodbrow, c. 1910. The isolated group of cottages in the middle distance is Denshaw Fold, a hamlet much older than the village which developed around Christ Church to the left. Denshaw Vale calico printing works was an important concern that employed a workforce of 150 in the late nineteenth century. It derived some of its coal from workings on the hillside on which the photographer was standing.

Delph from Carrcote, c. 1910. This largely nineteenth-century village is seen from the north-west. As was the case with all Saddleworth's valley villages, textile factories were a strong – and smoky – presence in the settlement. In 1937 Saddleworth Urban District Council accepted tenders for the building of forty-five houses on the fields in the foreground. Council houses were built at several locations in Saddleworth at this period to relieve a shortage of affordable and sanitary dwellings.

King Street, Delph, c. 1900. The main street of Delph is on, or near, the line of a routeway between Lancashire and Yorkshire that has been used since Roman times. Of the buildings in view, that on the extreme left is the Manchester and County Bank, erected on the site of a school in the 1880s. Beyond the carts near the bridge across the River Tame, is the chimney of Eagle Mill. St Thomas's church (1765) is on the skyline. The relative width of King Street made it ideal for public gatherings. Probably the most agitated were in 1895 when strikers from a local mill clashed with police.

King Street, Delph, *c.* 1895. The man standing in the doorway of this smith shop on King Street is probably its proprietor, Mr Bray. Soon after the photograph was taken his premises were demolished, apparently to improve access to an adjacent street.

King Street, *c.* 1905. The inhabitants of Delph have never been short of watering-holes. Three public houses can be seen in this view from the bridge over the River Tame. On the right is the Rose and Crown, put up in around 1890 on the site of a much earlier building. In the centre is the Packhorse, dating from the 1740s and ceasing to be a pub in 1914. The building with the advertisement hoarding on its side, is the Swan; established in around 1800, this was the largest inn to be found in the village.

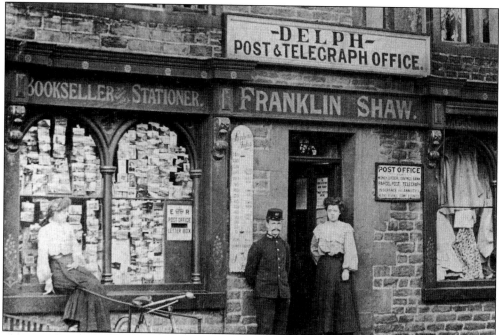

Post office, King Street, Delph, c. 1905. This was one of the first post offices to be established in Saddleworth. In the 1820s letters would arrive here each day at 10.30 a.m. and be collected at 4.30 p.m. As the sign to the right of the door testifies, the range of services had expanded greatly by the early twentieth century. Note the numerous commercial postcards in the window, a measure of how popular this means of communication was at the time.

Delph Bridge, c. 1910. The centuries-old ford at the end of King Street was eventually displaced by this handsome bridge. The River Tame is not always so placid as depicted here. In August 1857, for example, a thunderstorm produced a surge of water which flooded much of the village; an identical thing happened in July 1872.

Tame Valley near Wallhill, *c.* 1910. Bailey Mill and nearby buildings at New Delph can be seen at the top right of the photograph. Paralleling each other along the valley floor are the main road from Brownhill to Delph (1867) and the branch railway between the same points (1851). The bridge over the second mentioned was erected in 1893 to replace two level-crossings, which had been shown to be dangerous in 1888 when a train smashed into a horse and cart.

Barley Bridge, Delph, *c.* 1900. This spans the River Tame near Delph village. Its name suggests that it was built to provide employment for operatives at the local mills thrown temporarily out of work by slumps in trade.

Dobcross, *c.* 1870. Lined by houses built in the nineteenth century, when this old road was improved, Woods Lane sweeps up the hillside into the centre of Dobcross. Dominating the photograph is Walk Mill, its name recalling the ancient process of felting and thickening woollen cloth by treading or 'walking' it. According to Ammon Wrigley, the chimney of this mill was notorious for volcanic eruptions of soot, these invariably taking place on the Dobcross washing-day.

Dobcross Square, *c.* 1905. A memorial was erected here in August 1901 to Doctor Walter Henry Fox Ramsden. A combination of drinking fountain and base for a lantern, the memorial was made of Aberdeen granite and was funded by public subscription. Its existence was testimony to the great esteem in which this talented and dedicated individual was held in this village, where he had had a medical practice between 1864 and his death in 1900.

Dobcross from Ladcastle Road, c. 1910. Standing-out at the western edge of the village is Holy Trinity church, built in 1787. Strikingly modern in comparison is the detached house, 'Craigmont', which had recently been completed in the fields to the right. Running across the valley side below this is Dobcross New Road, built in 1865 to replace the indirect and steep route between Uppermill and Delph through the centre of Dobcross. By the River Tame in the foreground is a sewage works which is shown under construction on p. 95.

Uppermill, c. 1905. The extent to which this village once relied on factory-based industry is evident in this photograph taken from Brownhill. Perhaps the best-known legend in Saddleworth concerns the actions of elves and fairies who, in order to prevent the building of Saddleworth church on Brownhill, twice removed its stones to the site eventually adopted at the head of Pickhill Clough.

Uppermill, c. 1930. The chimney of Buckley New Mill is the vantage for this view of the centre of the village. In the top right of the photograph is The Square. Until growing road traffic in the twentieth century made the practice too inconvenient, this large space was the regular venue for the annual Whit Friday and Wakes Holiday festivities. The building in the top left of the photograph is Damhead Mill which survives today as a development of flats called Willow Bank.

Uppermill, *c.* 1900. Before the motor age it would have been common to see livestock being herded through the streets of Saddleworth's villages. Contributing to these movements were the cattle fairs that for long were held in Uppermill, one in Whitsun week, the other on the first Wednesday in October. At extreme right is the Waggon Inn, an erstwhile beerhouse dating from the mid-nineteenth century. Across the road is Ebenezer Chapel which had been built in the 1870s on the site of its predecessor of 1807.

Uppermill from Gellfield Lane, *c.* 1930. New housing on Heathfields Road is evidence of the steady expansion of Uppermill during the twentieth century. The large detached building nearby is Heathfields House. This dates from around 1820, some thirty years after its builder, the woollen manufacturer, John Platt, had finished the adjacent Heathfield Mill. At the near side of the lodge that fed the latter's waterwheel is the associated Heathfields Dyeworks, likewise since demolished.

Greenfield from Station Brow, *c. 1900*. Chew Valley Road runs through what is very clearly an industrial village. Dominating the foreground is Wellington Mill. Founded in 1853, this was typical of many of the later Saddleworth mills in being built to manufacture cotton products; it converted to wool in the 1930s. Beyond the railway and to the left of the terraces of houses on Berry Street, is another mill, Kinders, built in around 1800 for woollen manufacture.

Chew Valley Road, Greenfield, *c. 1910*. Wellington Mill is now seen from the eastern side against a backdrop of Wharmton Hill. This area of Greenfield is known as Frenches. Apart from being the site of one of the first mills in Saddleworth, Frenches was the point where an old packhorse road crossed the River Tame. The tall building on the hillside just above the end of the road was known familiarly as 'the lighthouse' for reasons obvious to anyone passing along the road at night.

Greenfield, *c.* 1900. The large building on the left of this view is the Greenfield Conservative Club; opened in 1894, its florid late-Victorian styling contrasts with the workaday look of the adjoining terraces. Just visible on the lower slopes of Wharmton Hill is Wharmton Tower, a mansion built in the 1860s and used as a military hospital during the First World War.

Greenfield, *c.* 1930. On the right is the Conservative Club. The bridge carried the Stalybridge-Diggle railway line across Chew Valley Road between the mid-1880s and the mid-1970s. In the distance is Road End.

Road End, Greenfield, *c.* 1900. The probable explanation for the name of this location is that after being completed to this point in around 1810, there followed a pause of some ten years before Chew Valley Road was continued eastwards. The King William The Fourth public house was built in the 1820s. A minor event in its history was the holding of a dinner there in 1896 to commemorate the erection of the first street lamp in the village. Children gather around this lamp and its decorative stone base.

Greenfield from Horsforth Road, *c.* 1900. Built in 1865, for cotton spinning, this was one of several mills whose establishment in Greenfield fostered the rapid growth of the village; it was demolished in 1979. Across the field is Road End. The long, three-storey building here is Piccadilly where, in February 1857, the Greenfield Co-operative Society opened their first shop; the site is now occupied by the car park of the King William the Fourth public house.

Shaw Hall Bank Road, c. 1900. This was built in the early 1850s by the Whiteheads of Royal George Mills to connect their premises with Greenfield village. It became a public thoroughfare in 1855 when acquired by the Staley Turnpike Trust to form the northern end of their new tollroad from Stalybridge via Wellihole. This view is relatively unchanged today, although the house on the left by the junction with Oaklands Road has long since been demolished.

Royal George from Wharmton Hill, c. 1905. Adjacent to the long-vanished railway sidings near Oaklands Road are houses lining Shaw Hall Bank Road. At extreme right is Christ Church, completed in the early 1850s. Its building was financed by the firm of R.R. Whitehead and Brothers, whose Royal George Mills are marked by the tall chimney not far from the church. Once renowned for the flags they produced, Whiteheads became best known for manufacturing felts. The mills have now closed, along with the majority of the factories whose chimneys dominate Mossley in the background.

Grasscroft from Wharmton Hill, c. 1935. The ancient hamlet of Grasscroft is barely discernible among the large number of modern, red-brick houses that have sprung up alongside Oldham Road. The tide of suburbia rises to the neighbouring settlement of Lydgate. Just to the left of St Anne's church at Lydgate is the water tower that was built in 1910 as part of a scheme to bring a mains supply to the area in view for the first time; it was demolished in 1975. Also now vanished are Summershades Pleasure Gardens in the bottom right of the photograph; these were once a very popular venue for local outings.

Oldham Road, Grasscroft, c. 1935. The spur to the growth of Grasscroft and Lydgate in the twentieth century was the improvement in 1926 of the main road from Uppermill to Oldham Ribbon development of housing took place all along the widened stretch from Brookway to Lydgate crossroads. The result was a type of landscape new to Saddleworth, one designed with the private car in mind.

Two

Farmsteads
and Hamlets

Rough Meadow Head, *c.* 1910. This farmstead stands by the ancient path from Swan Meadow to Heys, just west of Delph. Unusual features are several recesses cut into an outside wall. The function of these 'bee-boles' was to protect hives from wind. Bee-keeping was once quite common in Saddleworth, the honey either sweetening a household's diet or being sold to generate welcome additional income.

Knarr Clough, Thurston Clough Road, *c.* 1910. This eighteenth-century building near Delph is little changed today. Until a new and less steeply graded route was adopted further down the hillside around 1800, the road past this cottage had been part of the Wakefield and Austerlands turnpike, once one of the most important links between Lancashire and Yorkshire. This particular stretch may well have been the work of the famous road builder, John Metcalf, 'Blind Jack of Knaresborough'.

Thurston Clough, *c.* 1910. This landscape of scattered farmsteads and weavers' cottages just south-west of Delph recalls the intermingling of agriculture and home-based industry that was the essence of the domestic textile system in Saddleworth before the factory age. Among the buildings visible is Set Stones, the three-storeyed house with smoking chimney alongside Thurston Clough Road. Directly above this in the photograph is Valenciennes, one of many examples of combined house and barn to be found in the district.

Husteads Farm, *c*. 1900. A splendid evocation of a typical Saddleworth farmstead of the eighteenth century. The location is Wall Hill Clough, near Tamewater, Dobcross. In the 1841 Census two families are recorded as residing here. One comprised James Buckley, his wife and their eight children. Listed as a merchant, Mr Buckley was the owner of the nearby Husteads Mill.

Brimmy Croft, Denshaw, *c.* 1920. Built in the mid-eighteenth century, this building typifies the Saddleworth farmhouse of that period. A tannery used to be located here, evidence of which is the tan yard and associated pits that were included in a description of the property when it was advertised for sale in 1762.

Slack Head, *c.* 1900. Seen from the lane that connected it with Fernlee, this was one of a number of farmsteads established on the hillsides overlooking Greenfield. The following account dates from 1871: 'A visit to the places named Fernlee and Slack Head will help repay the toil. On the slope of Alphin will be found many specimens of the primitive inhabitant, soil of the soil, ruddy of complexion, strong in bone and muscle, and odorous of turf smoke.'

Slack Head, *c.* 1930. This building is now viewed from the slopes of Alphin Pike. Almost 1,000ft above sea level, it was typical of numerous old Saddleworth farmsteads in being sited midway between a valley bottom and the moorland plateau that covers much of the district. When villages developed in the valleys, so the hillsides lost favour as places to live and many of the dwellings there gradually disappeared. Slack Head's turn for abandonment came in around 1965.

Fernlee, Greenfield. *c.* 1930. This is one of the oldest known settlement sites in Saddleworth. An Adam de Fernlee is listed in the Poll Tax returns of 1379. Later, Fernlee became a hamlet of handloom weavers but at the date of this photograph it was a small farming community. The growing popularity of hiking during the twentieth century induced a number of hillside farms to offer refreshments.

Higher Kinders, Greenfield, *c.* 1910. This is one of the finest examples of a domestic weaving settlement in Saddleworth. Originating in the mid-seventeenth century, it was extended over the years in accord with the requirements of the half dozen or so families who lived there at any given time. Evident are the 'takin-in' steps which allowed access to the workroom without the need to traverse the living quarters on the lower floors.

Saddleworth Fold, *c.* 1880. This is possibly the oldest hamlet in the district. Angus Reach, a newspaper correspondent who visited in 1849, left a vivid description: 'From Uppermill we proceeded to a cluster of houses occupied by several families, who were at once spinners, weavers and farmers. The hamlet was a curious irregular clump of old-fashioned houses, looking as if they had been flung accidentally together. The man whose establishment we had come to see did not at all approve of the new-fangled mill system, and liked the old-fashioned way of joining weaving and farming much better. In the room above us were looms and spinning jennies. Weaving and spinning formed the chief occupation of the family – they attended to the cows and to the dairy in their leisure time'.

Millcroft, *c.* 1900. This hamlet in the Castleshaw Valley has associations with the childhood of the famous Saddleworth writer and historian, Ammon Wrigley. In 1868, when aged seven, he moved with his parents to the house on the right. Three years later, the family took up residence in the building adjoining, before settling shortly afterwards in the house that is partly obscured by trees in this photograph. Such 'flitting' was commonplace at a period when accommodation was generally rented and a family's possessions few.

Wharmton, Dobcross, *c*. 1900. Exemplifying the type of household which used to be found at this long-established weavers' hamlet was that of William Shaw, whom the Census of 1841 records as having been a clothier with five children. Wharmton is best known for its school, however. This was founded in 1729 when Ralph Hawkyard died and left £200 to fund a school and its master. English, Latin and Greek were the main subjects taught until this tiny establishment closed in 1883.

Tamewater, *c*. 1890. These ancient cottages stood off Bank Lane, between Wall Hill Road and Delph New Road. They were demolished in the early twentieth century. Note the traditional flag-stone roof and, in the foreground, the large and well-tended vegetable garden.

Looking north from Grains Road, c. 1900. In the centre of the photograph is the hamlet of Slackcote. Dominating this hamlet is the woollen mill at which almost all of its inhabitants worked. Built in 1781, Slackcote Mill was taken over by Robert Byrom in the 1850s. He had been born in 1815 at Bankfield, the house visible in the left foreground. In 1870 Mr Byrom had accumulated sufficient wealth to build the large Brookland Lodge near the mill. Robert Byrom's progression from relative poverty to affluence is emblematic of the great changes the textile industry brought to Saddleworth.

Slackcote, c 1900. To house the average of eighty or so employees at Byrom's mill, terraced housing was provided at the hamlet and near Brookland Lodge. The Byroms were keen cricketers and a prospective hand would have a distinct advantage if he could offer skills as batsman or bowler.

Three
Work and Industry

Col's Coal Pit, Delph. Also known as 'Colts Pit,' this was one of the locations at which the coal measures between Delph and Denshaw were worked. Around 1800 coal was conveyed from here to Diggle by packhorse, for use by the navvies building Standedge Canal Tunnel. The coal from this pit was so hard that it would crackle and fly when burned, a trait that gave rise to the descriptive term 'Colts bullets'. The photograph dates from the temporary re-opening of the pit during a national coal strike in 1912.

Carr Barn Farm, *c.* 1900. This stood about midway between Uppermill and Greenfield on the open expanse of Carr Fields. It once doubled as a beer house, the proprietor of which was prosecuted in 1868 for selling beer on Good Friday. Carr Barn was demolished in the 1950s when an estate of council housing was built on Carr Fields.

Carr Fields, *c.* 1920. Bringing in the hay near Carr Barn Farm. The trees in the middle distance mark the edge of what in the 1960s became Churchill Playing Fields. Houses along Beech Avenue now cover the open land in the foreground of the photograph.

Greenfield Valley, c. 1900. A rare photograph of that ancient and staple activity in Saddleworth, sheep rearing. It would be impossible to graze sheep at this particular location today as it lies under the water of Dovestone reservoir, completed in 1966. Many of the trees visible in Chew Valley in the background have also disappeared, only stumps remaining of what used to be extensive plantations.

Pig Club, Dobcross, c. 1910. The men seen here near Bankfield Cottages, Wallhill Road, are studying the pigs they have jointly purchased and the meat from which they will eventually share. Such mutual enterprise also allowed funds to be raised to compensate any member of the club, should he lose an animal through illness or accident.

Bridge House, Dobcross, *c.* 1900. Built in around 1790, this building is best known as the birthplace of Henry Platt (1793-1842). A blacksmith by trade, he built woollen carding engines in the single-storey workshop to the right in the photograph. He went on to found what became the largest firm of textile machinery makers in the world.

HARTFORD NEW WORKS

At their peak, the premises of Platt Brothers on Featherstall Road in Oldham, five miles west of Dobcross, had a workforce of 15,000. Very little remains today of this extensive site.

Hull Mill, 1987. Mills have disappeared from the Saddleworth landscape at a steady rate. The turn of Hull Mill, near Delph, came in around 1990. Latterly a bleaching and dyeing concern, it had been built in 1787 as one of the first cotton factories in the district.

Tunstead Clough Mill, c. 1900. Alfred Winterbottom is seen delivering milk to this woollen mill, built in the 1780s. Nothing now remains of the mill itself although the lodge that supplied its waterwheel has been retained for private fishing.

Johnny Mill, c. 1890. This stood by Hull Brook in the Castleshaw Valley. Built in 1787, it processed wool until closed in the 1880s. Being near the site of two reservoirs which Oldham Corporation had just begun to construct, in 1887 the vacant building was adopted by a 'mission' which had been instituted by the Methodists of Delph to cater for the hundreds of navvies employed on this project. In addition to holding regular services here, the mission arranged entertainment and lectures on practical topics. The culmination was an exhibition in February 1889 of work done by the navvies. The main exhibit was a clock made of 2,346 pieces of wood without the use of nails or glue. On opening the exhibition, the Delph industrialist Mr Mallalieu eulogised the navvies as 'good neighbours and good citizens'.

Waters Mill, c. 1885. This stood a short distance from Johnny Mill. Also known as Nield Mill, it was built in around 1790 and closed around the date of the photograph. That it looks as much a domestic as an industrial building is because it was constructed during the transition from producing woollen cloth in the home to manufacturing it in factories. Only the mill's lodge survives today.

Filter House, Castleshaw, *c.* 1920. Water from the Castleshaw Upper Reservoir was treated in this building before being fed along a pipeline for four and a half miles to Oldham. Emphasising the scale of the engineering involved in the Castleshaw waterworks project, was the fact that a tunnel a mile and a half in length was bored to take this pipeline from Delph to Strinesdale. Built in 1915, the filter house was demolished in 1971.

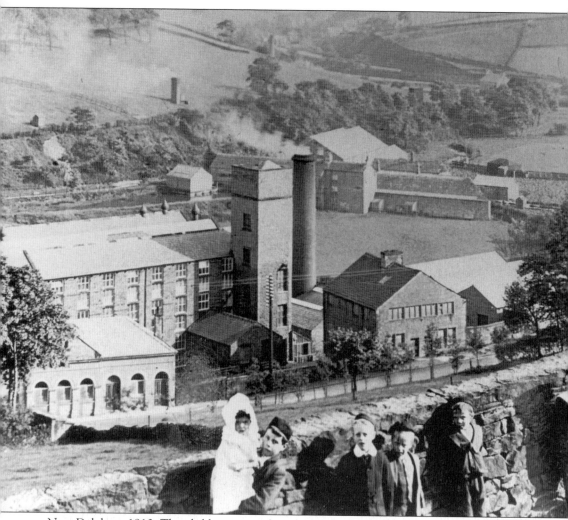

New Delph, c. 1910. The children are gathered on Stoneswood Road. In the middle distance is Gatehead Mill; built in 1781 alongside the River Tame, this was the earliest cotton mill in Saddleworth. Prominent in the foreground is Bailey Mill, a woollen factory established in 1865. This mill was at the forefront of a wave of labour unrest that swept through Saddleworth in the 1890s. The dispute over pay and lack of union rights was resolved only at the cost of much bitterness and violence, which included open conflict with the police.

Husteads Mill, c. 1900. Built in the late 1780s this woollen mill is viewed over the lodge that supplied its water. Wall Hill Clough was one of several tributaries of the River Tame in Saddleworth to be used by early water-powered textile mills, four of these being established along the half-mile length of the clough. Husteads Mill fell out of use soon after this photograph was taken and only bits of masonry remain today to mark the site.

Wallhill Cough, c. 1900. Below Husteads Mill were two other industrial buildings. Reflected in its lodge is Fozzards Mill, a dyeworks established in the 1830s. Later, it was incorporated into Bankfield Mill a large steam-powered woollen factory. Bankfield was built by the Hirst family, wealthy landowners in nearby Dobcross and whose tomb, decorated by stone panels depicting aspects of the woollen industry, is to be found at Saddleworth church. Both mills have been demolished.

Buckley New Mill, c. 1900. This woollen mill in Uppermill village was built in stages between 1840 and 1870. From 1876 until its closure in 1979 it was run by the woollen manufacturing firm, J.F. & C. Kenworthy, one of the last of many companies of this kind to have existed in Saddleworth. Pollution from mill chimneys was recognized as being a significant problem in the district in the late nineteenth and early twentieth centuries and the local council was ever on the watch for illegal emissions of 'black smoke', although successful prosecutions were few.

The chimney seen pouring out smoke in the previous photograph is depicted under repair in around 1930. This structure is one of the handful of mill chimneys that still exist in Saddleworth, having been retained as a 'feature' when new housing obliterated much of the rest of Buckley New Mill in the 1990s.

Buckley New Mill, Uppermill, November 1950. One of the many activities undertaken in the local woollen mills was that entrusted to Fred Hudson by J.F. & C. Kenworthy Limited. As a loom-tuner he was required to rectify faults reported by weavers and also adjust looms to accept new 'patterns'. A number of shuttles, essential features of the machinery Mr Hudson tended, can be seen stored in the bottom left of the photograph.

Eagle Mill fire. All was confusion and farce when at 12 noon on Friday 12 October 1906 a fire began at Eagle Mill in Delph village. The mill was devoid of fire-fighting equipment of any sort, while what hose-piping that could be located was rendered virtually useless through the couplings being of several different sizes; low pressure in the village water mains added to these problems. The mill was completely destroyed and a relief fund had to be set up for the many employees deprived of work by the disaster.

Greenfield Mill, 1914. Once the largest woollen mill in Saddleworth, by the early part of the twentieth century it had declined into the role of bleaching cotton waste. On 9 March 1914 10,000 pounds of cotton wool were in the finishing department when a machine caught fire. The finishing department was destroyed and 100 employees were thrown out of work. Prompted by such regular devastation, in 1919 Saddleworth Urban District Council reached an agreement with Mossley brigade, whereby fire cover would be provided to the district in return for an annual sum raised by a penny rate.

Wellington Mill fire, Greenfield, 5 March 1955. A hundred firemen and a dozen appliances could do little to control a spectacular blaze that virtually destroyed one of the largest mill-buildings in Saddleworth. The photograph was taken from just below Station Brow where large numbers of spectators congregated to watch.

The aftermath of the fire viewed the following day from Chew Valley Road, which had been blocked by the collapse of tons of masonry. The mill would be rebuilt, although the upper two of its five storeys were not replaced.

Diggle New Mill, c. 1910. This mill was built in a remote location near the head of the Diggle Valley, its access road crossing Diggle Brook on this elegant bridge. At the time of the photograph the mill's proprietors would sometimes use a carrier pigeon to communicate with their other factory in Micklehurst, four miles to the south.

Diggle New Mill. When built in 1847, this woollen mill was not provided with the usual steam engine to power its machinery. Instead, for reasons that still remain a mystery, a waterwheel was installed, so gargantuan that only Laxey wheel in the Isle of Man was larger in the United Kingdom. It had a diameter of just under 65ft, a width of 7ft, and 192 buckets, each with a capacity of 36 gallons; the horsepower produced was 140. The photograph shows the wheel in the course of demolition in December 1924.

Grotton Brickworks, *c.* 1950. The Lancashire and Yorkshire Fire Clay Works was founded in around 1860. Clay was quarried on the adjacent hillside and brought to the site by a short, gravity-powered railway. Bricks were far from being the only product, as the pipes visible in the photograph demonstrate. Indeed, in the 1870s tiles, chimney-tops and flue covers were among the many items being manufactured here. The close proximity of large towns such as Oldham and Ashton provided a ready market. The works closed in around 1980 and housing now covers the site.

Chew Reservoir, *c.* 1910. Between 1908 and 1914 a reservoir was built at the head of Chew Valley, near Greenfield. At the peak some 550 men worked at the construction site, the small group illustrated being among them. Conditions were hard at this bleak location, 1,600ft up in treeless moorland. Relief was often sought in alcohol. In April 1911 one navvy became so inebriated that, incapable of finding his bed he lay down in a stream instead, promptly falling asleep.

Several rail-mounted steam cranes were used at the Chew Reservoir site. Their main role was to remove material that was excavated to provide a watertight core in the dam. The 'gutter' was a dangerous place in which to work. The most serious accident there was in December 1908 when a navvy died after hitting a cartridge of gelignite with his pick.

Chew Tram Road, *c.* 1908. A 3ft gauge contractor's line brought construction materials to Chew Reservoir from exchange sidings with the Stalybridge-Diggle main line railway at Micklehurst. One of several wooden trestle bridges, by which gullies were crossed en route, is seen here. The location would appear to be near Dacres, Greenfield.

Charnel, Chew Valley, *c.* 1908. Around one mile from the reservoir site, the tram-road was taken up the side of Chew Valley by the inclined plane visible in this photograph. A steam winch at the summit raised wagons a vertical height of 525ft. Official visitors were conveyed between Micklehurst and the foot of the incline in the special coach seen here; workmen had to make do with wagons furnished with back-to-back seating under roofs of tin.

Dobcross Sewage Works, *c.* 1895. These workmen are helping build a sewage works, one of four such installations constructed in Saddleworth at this period. A comprehensive sewage scheme had been forced on the local authority by the West Riding County Council, which was concerned by the polluted state of the River Tame. Construction at Dobcross lasted from 1894 to 1896. The site is now occupied by a garden centre.

Delph, *c.* 1910. The village fish dealer poses outside the 'White Lion' public house. Robert Brown, whose name is on the inn sign, was licensee here between 1903 and 1930. The now demolished building immediately behind the cart stood at the corner of Denshaw Road and High Street. Overlooking the High Street, at far left, are Bell Buildings. These were constructed in 1880 on the site of the Blue Bell, which in the late eighteenth century was probably the most important inn in Delph.

54

Road-menders, Greenfield, 1898. A gang of road-menders, foreman on the right, pose for the camera. Their tools seem rudimentary for such a hard physical job. The location is not easy to determine, but is probably the lane up to Mount Pleasant Farm, south of Greenfield.

King Street, Delph, *c.* 1885. John Brierley, watch and clockmaker of Delph, is to be found listed in a commercial directory of 1866. As this photograph was taken nearly twenty years later, evidently his business was successful. The wooden toys in the window were perhaps a profitable sideline. Now a private house, this building looks much the same today.

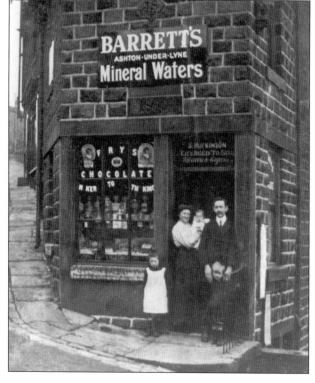

Station Brow, Greenfield, *c.* 1910. The Hopkinson family pose outside their corner shop. Much of their trade would have come from users of the railway station that was built further up the hill in 1849, a minor example of how railways stimulated the local economy. Although the shop closed in the 1970s, the date stone and the curious stone relief of a face above this can both still be seen.

56

High Street, Uppermill, *c.* 1910. Small shops proliferated in Uppermill during the nineteenth century as its population grew and the local economy expanded. Fryers druggists was one such business. The photograph can be dated to after 1894, as this was the year when the Saddleworth branch of St John's Ambulance Association, advertised in the shop window, was formed.

Walters' butchers shop, corner of High Street and Bridge Street, *c.* 1930. Herbert Walters is seen outside his shop. He had been born at Belvoir Castle, Nottinghamshire in 1880, son of the head gamekeeper of the Duke of Rutland – good background for the trade of butcher he adopted in Saddleworth.

Diggle Co-op, Sam Road, Diggle, *c.* 1900. In 1868 the Diggle Co-operative Society opened the premises seen here. The society enthusiastically applied the principle of self-help that was at the heart of the co-operative movement. When, in 1887, it was proposed to ban credit in the Sam Road store, a speaker from the Co-operative Wholesale Society applauded the idea: 'for it is much better for working men to be two weeks ahead of their wages than two weeks behind (hear, hear!)'.

Chew Valley Road, Greenfield, *c.* 1910. The shop visible on the right of the photograph was opened in around 1860 by the Greenfield Co-operative Society. Business was good, to the extent that in 1879 a three-storeyed building was erected directly opposite to house new drapery and butchery departments. Also incorporated in the new building was a large hall in which social functions and, from 1892, night-classes were held.

King Street, Delph, *c.* 1900. George Mellor, window cleaner, is at work on buildings near the Swan Inn, which can just be seen on the right. Rising above the roofline is the tower of the Wesleyan Chapel, a building erected in the 1890s and demolished in the 1950s.

Castleshaw Roman Fort. The first properly organized excavations here took place in the summers of 1907 and 1908. The work was under the supervision of Samuel Andrew and William Lees who had purchased the site for this purpose. With the help of five labourers they excavated much of Agricola's Fort of AD 79 and all of the associated *fortlet* that had been built in around AD 105.

Four
In Uniform

King Street, Delph *c*. 1916. In what today would be called a public relations exercise, a German field gun captured at Loos, France, in September 1915 is displayed by the Army. The building on the right is now occupied by the village newsagent.

Volunteers' Encampment, Uppermill, 1879. The 34th West Yorkshire Rifle Volunteers were formed in 1860. Saddleworth was within their area and the local headquarters were at Dobcross, with companies at Delph and Lydgate. An encampment was held on Pickhill Fields between 28 May and 4 June 1879 and around 130 tents were pitched. A housing estate and junior school now occupy the site.

The Commanding Officer at the encampment was Major Collins. He kept a tight rein on proceedings. An example of this was his dispatch one evening of pickets to extricate men from the public houses in Uppermill before they could become drunk.

Posed against a backdrop of Uppermill village are Major Collins, officers and visitors. The feeling of informality was appropriate to an event that, apart from sporadic drill and parades, was almost a social occasion. One volunteer recorded his impressions of this aspect: 'We had even more visitors to tea than we had to dinner. After tea was over the band commenced playing dancing music and in a very short time the field was almost covered with dancers.'

This building served as the mess house for the encampment. According to one participant, the men were well fed: 'Dinner consisted of the following per man. A pint of broth, half a pound of boiled beef, potatoes, bread and a pint of beer. I relished the broth and the beef very much and I can honestly say that I never tasted better broth.'

Military Hospital, Greenfield, Summer 1918. Photographed near Ashway Gap House are some of the patients and nurses who were in occupancy of this building between October 1915 and July 1919. Having aroused the displeasure of the War Office by frequenting Greenfield public houses each evening, in 1916 the residents were subjected to a strict curfew. During the Second World War the house accommodated soldiers of a different kind, Italian prisoners of war.

Ashway Gap House is seen as it was between the wars. It was a creation of the Saddleworth architect, George Shaw. He was commissioned in around 1850 to design a hunting lodge for the Oldham industrialist, John Platt. Despite being surrounded by moorland ideal for grouse shooting, it was little used for its intended purpose and stayed empty for long periods. It was demolished in 1981.

Uppermill, September 1919. A poignant moment in Saddleworth's history. On the same day as many servicemen returned home from war a ceremony was held in The Square to unveil a memorial to those who had not. Two hundred and ninety-six from Saddleworth died in the trenches, fifty-seven of these having lived in Uppermill. Here the frontage of the Wesleyan Chapel provides a convenient vantage for the participants.

The memorial was a modest affair and was soon removed. The angel still exists, now adorning a headstone in the lower graveyard at Saddleworth church.

Dobcross Brass Band, 1911. Saddleworth has been described as the cradle and centre of the brass band movement. Dobcross Band, formed in 1875, was one of several to be established in the district. The pride evident in the faces of this gathering of players near Platt Lane was reflected in the growing success of the band. A high point was their winning, in 1935, of the prestigious contest at Belle Vue in Manchester. At the time of the photograph virtually all the members of the band lived in Dobcross and it was their proud boast they could assemble themselves for a practice in one hour flat.

Home Guard, Delph, c. 1943. Seen on King Street on an unidentified occasion are some of Saddleworth's Local Defence Volunteers. Part of the Duke of Wellington's Regiment, the Saddleworth Home Guard was organized into four companies, based at Uppermill, Springhead, Denshaw and Greenfield.

Chew Reservoir, c. 1943. Mr W.W. Robinson, a member of the Waterworks' Detachment of the Home Guard, is seen here in his uniform. He was reservoir keeper at Chew for forty years, 1914-1954 inclusive.

Police station, Dobcross, *c.* 1924. Saddleworth gained its first police force in 1856 when the district was placed under the ambit of the West Riding Constabulary. The main 'county constabulary station' was established at Woolroad. Standing in front of this building is Superintendent Prosser. He also acted as churchwarden at Holy Trinity, Dobcross, between 1902 and 1905.

Woolroad, *c.* 1890. In 1869 the Woolroad station was visited by Captain Elgin, the Government Inspector of Police. He remarked that he had never encountered a division with a force so small in relation to the area covered. At that date the establishment comprised a superintendent, a sergeant and eight constables. To judge from this photograph taken outside the station twenty or so years later, the shortfall in staffing was remedied only gradually.

Five
Buildings

Junction Inn, Denshaw, *c.* 1905. Built in around 1805, this was a posting inn, from which travellers on the Oldham-Ripponden and Rochdale-Huddersfield turnpike roads that crossed here could hire post-chaises and horses. Alfred Schofield was licensee between 1901 and 1909. The photograph can be dated to after 1906, as there is no sign of the lamp that stood outside the inn until it was destroyed that year in an explosion in which the lighter's assistant was killed.

Bell Inn, Huddersfield Road, Delph, *c.* 1900. This was opened in 1794 to serve travellers on the adjacent Oldham-Huddersfield road. Originally called the New Inn, it was renamed at the beginning of the nineteenth century when William Bell was tenant. Many coaches stopped here: those doing so in the 1840s connected Manchester with Bradford, Huddersfield and Leeds. Soon after this, competition from the new trans-Pennine railways destroyed the Bell's coaching trade and by 1871 the inn had become a school. It is now a public house and restaurant.

Bell Yard, *c.* 1910. When, in the 1820s, the Bell was a posting house similar to the Junction at Denshaw, stabling was provided for forty-eight horses in Bell Yard. The building over the arch giving access to the yard was used first as a warehouse then as a dwelling; in 1938 Saddleworth Council condemned it as being unfit for human habitation.

Adjoining the Bell Inn is this substantial building. It was constructed in around 1820 by Edmund Buckley, tenant of Rasping Mill and the first proprietor of the New Inn. Recently it has been restored to very much the appearance it had when photographed in around 1880. Bell Yard is through the arch on the right.

White Lion, Delph, c. 1905. This public house was formed out of three dwellings in around 1790. It has continued as a pub ever since. The cottages lining Cobblers Hill on the right have not survived, however, Saddleworth Council ordering their demolition in November 1936. This photograph proves that old Saddleworth could be a grim place. In 1916 Ammon Wrigley described Delph as 'a bare, dreary-looking hole.'

The Floating Light, c. 1905. Built in the 1840s to cater for travellers on the Oldham-Huddersfield Road, this public house was sited 1,187ft above sea level on the Standedge ridge near Diggle. Joe Dyson was licensee between 1900 and 1916. His slogan was: 'I Joe lives here and sells good ale, come in and drink before it goes stale.' The building seen here was demolished soon after a new public house was opened alongside in 1940.

The Woolpack, c. 1900. This eighteenth-century building, adjacent to Woods Lane, Dobcross, became an inn in the 1770s. The Huddersfield-based brewery that purchased the property in 1914 replaced it twelve years later by a completely new public house. This was sited on the yard seen in the foreground which had formerly had been used for cattle auctions. The old Woolpack survives as a private house.

The Moorcock Inn, Greenfield. Originally a farmhouse, this building became an alehouse in around 1810 and a fully licensed inn in the 1840s. It was known popularly as 'Bill's o' Jack's', after its first proprietor, William Bradbury. Perhaps the most famous event in the history of Saddleworth was the murder, on 2 April 1832, of William Bradbury and his son at the inn, a crime that has never been solved.

Throughout the land, wherever news is read,
Intelligence of their sad death has spread;
Those now who talk of far-famed Greenfield hills
Will think of Bill o' Jack's and Tom o' Bill's.

J. PLATT.

The excess of violence used in the murders generated a great deal of morbid interest which remained attached to The Moorcock throughout its existence. This early twentieth-century postcard of articles associated with the event is an example of how this interest was exploited. Just a few days after the murders, members of the victims' families were charging visitors to view the scene of the crime.

W.  R.

£100 REWARD

WHEREAS on the night of April 2nd, 1832 William Bradbury and Tom Bradbury were done to death at the Moorcock Inn, on the Holmfirth Road, in the rish of Saddleworth, by some person or persons wn, the above Reward will be paid to any person or persons who will give information that will lead to the arrest of the said assassins, and the public are hereby warned that anyone giving shelter or aid to the said wanted person (or persons) are liable to severe punishment. Any information to be given to the nearest constable or to the undersigned,

WILLIAM MOON,

Home Office.

This poster was to prove as ineffective as all other attempts to identify who had committed the murders, and the mystery remains unsolved to this day. The Moorcock was closed in 1937 and was subsequently demolished.

Clarence Hotel, Greenfield, *c.* 1880. This was built in around 1861 in the 'vee' between Horsforth Road and Chew Valley Road. One aspect of a relatively uneventful history was that it was the meeting place of the Saddleworth Hunt during the 1870s. Augustus Bradbury was the licensee between 1862 and 1884.

The Hanging Gate, Huddersfield Road, Diggle, *c.* 1935. Known as the Gate Inn, when built in around 1801, this public house gained its present name around 1860. Something else it acquired was a reputation for the drunken behaviour of its customers; when the Saddleworth magistrates compiled a list of disorderly pubs in 1894, the Hanging Gate was on it. The building was rebuilt into the form seen here in 1926.

A distinctive feature of the Hanging Gate was its appropriate sign. Certainly in position by 1870, if not before, it was re-hung when the pub was reconstructed, taking a new position over Spurn Lane at the side of the building. It was photographed in around 1935.

St Mary's church, Greenfield, *c.* 1905. Built in 1875, this building is visible to the left. Its construction was financed by Richard Buckley, one of a family who had founded the Saddleworth Bank. Disappearing into the distance is the Greenfield-Holmfirth road. The promenaders on this would have been wise to be vigilant. A newspaper report of April 1910 highlighted The Motoring Danger here. Reportedly, cars were passing at 20mph; even 30mph had been alleged.

The Old Vicarage, Shepherds Green, Greenfield. The choir of St Mary's are seen on the day their new church was consecrated in 1875. From left to right, back row: Sam ?, John Rhodes, Arthur Radcliffe, Becket Byrom, William Schofield, Isaac Haytack, George Booth, Eli Hanson. Middle row: Ellen Radcliffe, ? Fallas, ? Lockwood, Nancy Wood, Annie Wood. Regrettably the names of those on the front row are illegible.

Saddleworth church, *c.* 1890. Apart from the presence of the two gentleman, this view of the seventeenth century stocks remains little changed today.

St Anne's church, Lydgate, *c.* 1900. This was built in 1788 in a plain, 'preaching-house' style. Outmoded, and battered by the elements at this exposed hilltop location, it was rebuilt between 1911 and 1913. A clock tower replaced the bell turret visible here. The clock itself was the gift of a Mr Cooper of Grasscroft Hall, in memory of his mother, and was illuminated each night at his expense.

Lydgate parsonage, *c.* 1890. In the mid-1830s, the reverend George Cowell of St Anne's church leased an estate at Manns near Shaw Hall Bank to the Whitehead Brothers of Royal George Mills. In exchange he obtained land on the outskirts of Lydgate village on which to build a parsonage. This was finished in 1839. Initially the building doubled as a farm, incorporating a hayloft, stable, pig-styes and a dovecote.

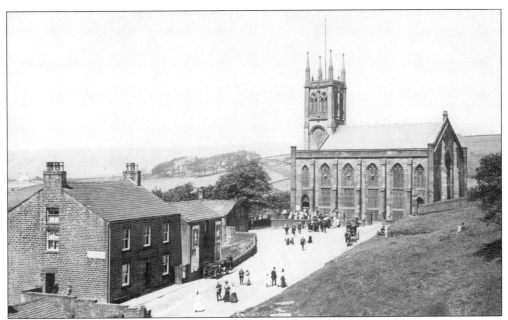

Saddleworth church, *c.* 1900. The first church was built on this site above Uppermill in around 1215. After much piecemeal rebuilding, by the early nineteenth century St Chad's was in decrepit condition. As the historian Colonel Howcroft put the matter, bills for its repair 'came in as regularly as the wheel came off the hearse, the clappers fell out of the bells and the water ran through the church roof'. Finally, in 1833, it was reconstructed, taking the form seen here. To the left, being passed by stragglers of a wedding party, is the Church Inn, opened in 1827.

Prominent in this view, taken around 1900, is the tower that was added to the rebuilt Saddleworth church in 1846. The ringers of the bells hung within won many contests round the north of England during the nineteenth century. Of the contests held at the church itself, possibly the greatest was in August 1875, although, regrettably, the first prize of £20 and a silk banner went to a team from outside the district. The semi-ruinous building to the right is part of Clerks Farm, so named as the parish clerks once resided here.

Wesleyan Chapel, Uppermill Square, *c.* 1900. Opened in 1813, this building was demolished almost exactly a century later, to be replaced by the chapel that stands on the site today. Being above the level of the surrounding ground, the graveyard of the old chapel was a hazard to health. Burials ceased in 1875 after Uppermill Local Board had complained that 'in certain seasons a liquid comes through the wall onto the adjoining land which is surrounded by buildings'.

St Chad's House, Uppermill, *c.* 1880. George Shaw (1810-1876) came from a line of yeoman farmers, master clothiers and industrialists, but his passion was for architecture. He applied this enthusiasm to the family home, reconstructing its interior in flamboyant style and embellishing its exterior with decorative gables and castellations. In 1920 the house was purchased by the Saddleworth Urban District Council and since 1984 has served as the village library.

St Chad's Chapel, *c.* 1920. George Shaw built this in the 1840s in the space between his home and High Street. Incorporated into the building were some of the materials he was accustomed to collect from properties he had been commissioned to renovate. Much of the chapel was demolished when the Manchester and County Bank – visible on the right – was built in 1881, the bulk of the remainder disappearing in the twentieth century.

Delph Lodge, *c.* 1880. Completed in 1803, this large house in elegant, neo-classical style was a visible expression of the wealth of its owner. James Lees had been a cotton manufacturer in Manchester before returning to Saddleworth to settle. Visible here is part of the extension that his son commissioned and in the dining room of which Handel's *Messiah* was performed each Christmas by the Saddleworth Musical Society.

Lower Brownhill House, *c.* 1910. This building is viewed from Uppermill village. Its tenant from around 1802 was John Rooth. He was a merchant who took a keen professional interest in the Huddersfield Canal, which was being built through Saddleworth at this time. In addition to becoming the first carrier on the canal, he was appointed its manager in 1801. In around 1806 Rooth built the Navigation Inn at Woolroad, Dobcross.

Dowry Castle, *c.* 1890. In 1867 John Gartside, a brewer from Ashton-under-Lyne, built a large house on a bleak hillside a mile or so north-east of Denshaw. The cost was £17,000. The money was poorly spent as the building was to be demolished only thirty years later. Its foundations can still be seen near Dowry Reservoir, built in the 1880s and the close proximity of which was the main reason why the house ultimately had to go.

Church Fields, Dobcross, *c.* 1900. Familiarly known as 'the house with knobs on', because of the stone finials on its gables, this building was the home of a yeoman in the seventeenth century. By the mid-eighteenth century it was occupied by the Lawtons, on whose energy and enterprise much of the development of Dobcross would depend. They were also a wealthy family; when Mary Lawton married in 1768 she was reputed to possess a fortune of £30,000.

St Chad's School, Church Road, Uppermill. This school was opened in 1863, the photograph – one of the earliest to be taken in Saddleworth – recording it a few years after this date. Being too small and remote, the school was replaced in 1883 by new premises on Lee Street in Uppermill village. The original building survives today as dwellings, although the expanse of Well Meadow to its rear was built over in the 1960s.

St Chad's School, Lee Street, Uppermill, 1908. The school football team is photographed in the school yard by Station Road. The majority of these pupils would have been 'half-timers', their weeks divided between attendance at school and work in the local mills. In 1911the headmaster lamented that teaching the upper two classes was very difficult as all but one pupil was a half-timer.

Lydgate School, c. 1865. Located by Stockport Road, this was built in 1767. It was rebuilt into its present form in 1869 and continued as a school until a new building elsewhere in the village replaced it in 1967.

Denshaw School, Delph Road, *c.* 1910. Adjacent to the cottages at Range is the school built by public subscription in 1824. Its first master was George Duckworth, who for a few years immediately beforehand had been in charge of a day school held in a private house elsewhere in Denshaw.

Council School, Uppermill, *c.* 1911. As the population of Saddleworth grew so the number of schools there increased. The Council School by Pickhill Fields is seen shortly after its opening in September 1911. Fifty years later it was subsumed into the present-day Saddleworth Comprehensive School. The original building has been retained as classrooms, refectory and community education centre.

Castleshaw School, c. 1890. This was founded in 1817. With her pupils in the photograph is Mrs Clayton who was schoolmistress here between 1853 and 1894. Her unhappy expression reflects the difficulties she encountered. As the number of families living in the Castleshaw Valley declined, so fewer and fewer children attended the school. Mrs Clayton's salary declined commensurately, with the result that she died in virtual poverty. The school struggled on until around 1913. The building is now a private house.

Castleshaw Open Air School, c. 1920. Once called Water Cote and subsequently Liftrey Dyke, this erstwhile farmhouse was given to the town of Oldham in 1916 for use as a school for disadvantaged children. Known as Castleshaw Open Air School, it accommodated around two dozen children in three dormitories. Relatives were allowed to visit every other Saturday. Now called the Castleshaw Centre, the building is still owned by Oldham Council.

Daisy Hill, Knarr Barn Lane, Thurston Clough, *c.* 1900. In 1798 this building became the Saddleworth Workhouse, replacing premises at Grange in the Castleshaw Valley. Such was the amount of destitution in the district that it quickly proved too small for the purpose. When a new workhouse was opened at Runninghill in 1816, Daisy Hill was sold and has been a private house ever since.

Runninghill Workhouse, c. 1895. This was opened in 1816. By the time of this photograph it was serving a variety of functions, including a hospital for the mentally ill and refuge for those too old and infirm to support themselves. On census night in 1891 there were sixty-six inmates, of ages ranging from six to eighty-two. Of these, two were described as 'imbecile' and one as 'paralytic'. In addition there were seventeen adults recorded as 'vagrants'. Being on a direct route between Lancashire and Yorkshire, Runninghill was often used as an overnight stop for men 'on the tramp'; in 1906 it was estimated that fifty such tramps were claiming relief at the workhouse each fortnight.

Workhouse staff and inmates, c. 1905. The Saddleworth workhouse acquired a reputation for two qualities that could easily have been contradictory, efficiency and kindness. The children there would seem to have been among the beneficiaries of this enlightened attitude. This was instanced in 1907 when the Guardians received a letter from the mother of a young girl who had been admitted when suffering from consumption and who subsequently died: 'I can scarcely express my gratitude for the way you treated my daughter. I shall always think of you and praise you for all you did.'

Mechanics' Institute, Delph, *c.* 1910. In 1883 the Delph Mechanics Institute took up residence in substantial new premises on Millgate. Costing £2,500, their centrepiece was a hall that could seat 580. In addition to being a venue for lectures and evening classes, the institute was a social centre for the village. For example, in November 1909 its hall was adapted as a temporary rink for roller-skating, while in 1918 the building was the home of the Star Picture Palace, an early cinema. The site is now a car park.

Terraces, Diggle, *c.* 1910. The second half of the nineteenth century left its mark on Saddleworth in the form of rows of stone-built dwellings, this being an urban style of architecture quite different from that which had hitherto been the norm locally. Huddersfield Road provides a good example of such a development. Occupying one of the buildings on the left behind the proud mothers is Diggle post office.

Cockleshell Cottage, *c.* 1900. Built in around 1747, this house derived its name from the seashells that were embedded in the wall separating it from Platt Lane. Almost deserted in this view, the latter had formed the principal route between Dobcross and Delph until a new road was built in the valley bellow in 1867.

Berry Street, Greenfield, *c.* 1910. Many houses were built in Saddleworth by its co-operative societies. The Greenfield society constructed a total of eighty-seven dwellings between 1876 and the 1920s. These twin terraces were put up between 1899 and 1901. Indicative that the Greenfield Co-op was not behind the times, was that eight of the houses seen here were equipped with bathrooms.

SADDLEWORTH PALACE

UPPERMILL
Nr. OLDHAM

Nightly at 7.15
Saturdays and Holidays at 6.15 and 8.30

Prices of Admission—
Balcony 1/9, Children 1/-
Stalls 1/-, Children 7d.

Booking Hours—Mon., Tues., Thur.
and Fri. 5.15 to 7.45, Sat. 11 to 12.30
2 to 4 and 5.15 to 8

**NOVEMBER
1957**

The Saddleworth Palace, High Street, Uppermill. This cinema was opened by the Milnsbridge Picture Palace Company in September 1913. The balcony could seat ninety, the stalls six hundred. The Palace is seen in its heyday, being decorated for the coronation of King George VI in 1937. After closure in 1959 the building was taken over by Central Garage, whose original premises can be glimpsed on the extreme left.

Saddleworth Palace programme, 1957. At this late date the cinema was still open six evenings a week and for matinees on Saturday. Films advertised included *Green for Danger*, with Trevor Howard and Alistair Sim, *Written on the Wind*, starring Rock Hudson and Lauren Bacall, and *The Road to Bali*, featuring Dorothy Lamour, Bing Crosby and Bob Hope. An advertisement in the brochure was for Watson's television engineers in Uppermill; something of an irony, as this new form of mass entertainment was about to kill the Palace.

Six

On the Move

Greenfield, *c*. 1910. Cycling became a popular activity in Saddleworth in the late nineteenth century. In 1893, for example, there is mention of a Saddleworth Cycling Union, while a tradition of holding an annual charity parade of cyclists in fancy dress had already begun by this date. A club for cyclists was formed in Greenfield in 1897 and it is possible that this photograph outside the Royal George Inn depicts one of their outings.

Wade Lock, Uppermill, *c.* 1900. The Huddersfield Canal was authorised in 1794, to link the town in its title with Ashton-under-Lyne. Effectively part of a railway company from the 1840s, it experienced a long, slow decline thereafter and by the date of this photograph the sight of a loaded narrow boat in Saddleworth would have been rare. Following a remarkable effort of restoration, the canal was reopened throughout in 2001.

Woolroad, *c.* 1880. The Huddersfield Canal reached here in 1799. Until the great tunnel from Diggle to Marsden was completed in 1811, goods were transhipped at this point for carting over Standedge. One of the buildings used in this activity stands on the left bank of the canal, its cantilevered roof overhanging the water; this warehouse survives today, painstakingly restored. Long-demolished, however, is the large warehouse in this view. In the mid-nineteenth century narrow boats called daily at Woolroad, conveying goods as far afield as Hull and London.

Also visible in the photograph above, this bridge carried the canal tow-path over the arm that served the warehouse. The stone pillar was positioned to protect the masonry of the bridge from horse tow-ropes and has been deeply scarred by these. The bridge was demolished in the 1940s, its site being marked today by a boat slip-way into the restored canal.

Saddleworth Station, *c.* 1910. A stopping train from Huddersfield is approaching. The waiting passengers would have been well-advised to buy tickets as the penalty for not doing so could be severe. In October 1851 one Joseph Taylor spent a night in the parish lock-up after travelling without a ticket from Saddleworth to Greenfield. Saddleworth Station closed in October 1968. Part of it survives as a private house.

Saddleworth Viaduct, *c.* 1930. Crossing this structure, which was built in 1849 to carry the Stalybridge-Huddersfield railway over Brownhill Vale, is a train about to stop at the nearby Saddleworth station. At extreme left is the Bar House, a café and shop that was demolished when Wool Road was widened in 1966. The building immediately below the locomotive was a council depot at this date but is now the Brownhill Countryside Centre.

Greenfield station staff, 1884. Two of the figures can be identified. Sitting in the centre is the stationmaster, William Woolley. Born in 1831, he had been a footman before joining the railway in the 1850s, and was stationmaster at Diggle prior to coming to Greenfield. Standing to the extreme left is William's relative, Percy Yates Woolley, born in 1870. At the present day this station has one member of staff, who works part time.

Standedge Tunnel, Diggle, *c.* 1960. The train is emerging from the last-built of three parallel tunnels that took the Stalybridge-Huddersfield railway under the Standedge ridge from Diggle to Marsden; each three miles in length, they opened in 1849, 1871 and 1894 respectively. The tank visible on the right supplied water to troughs just inside the tunnel in view and from which locomotives could replenish their tenders whilst in motion; no other tunnel in Britain was so equipped. In the foreground are the platforms of Diggle station, which was to close in 1968.

Standedge Tunnel, *c.* 1893. Construction of the third railway tunnel is seen in its final stages. Conditions and terms of work were hard for the navvies. In 1892, for example, each shift lasted from 7 a.m. to 6 p.m., for which payment was six shillings. Injuries were frequent and fatalities not uncommon. The presence of a resident surgeon was much valued in these circumstances and in October 1893 the workforce showed their appreciation by presenting Dr Aspinall with a purse of gold.

Ward Lane, Diggle. On 5 July 1923 a passenger train from Leeds collided with a goods train soon after leaving Standedge Tunnel. The driver of the goods train had misinterpreted the instructions of a signalman and as a result moved forward into the path of the express. Awaiting aid from the breakdown train visible to the left in the photograph is one of the two locomotives at the head of the express.

Spanned by the bridge carrying Ward Lane are several coaches of the unfortunate express. Four people died in the carnage.

Railway Smash Greenfield Aug 16th 1909 C.C.

Friezland accident. In 1886 a railway was opened from Diggle to Stalybridge, duplicating the existing line between those points along the opposite side of the Tame Valley. Known as the Micklehurst Loop, the new route was used mainly by freight traffic. One of the few regular passenger trains to follow it was the Huddersfield-Stockport service that on 10 August 1909 left the rails at Friezland, killing the driver and fireman. Excessive speed down the gradient from Greenfield was the probable cause.

The enterprise of the firm that produced this commemorative postcard was outmatched by that of the photographer who presented magic lantern views of the disaster the same evening at a cinema in Stalybridge.

Friezland, September, 1965. Approaching the scene of the accident of 1909 is a freight from the direction of Stalybridge. The line closed in October 1966, eventually being converted into a bridle-way. The train is leaving a short tunnel underneath the Greenfield-Mossley road.

Delph Donkey. Produced in around 1900 as a commercial postcard, this cartoon recalls the tribulations of travel on the Delph Donkey, the branch railway from Uppermill to Delph that opened in 1851. In February of 1858 'An Inhabitant of Delph' wrote to a local newspaper to complain: 'You enter the carriage at Delph station and before you are aware, a number of coal or luggage trucks which have been fetched from a siding, come thump up against the passenger carriage and you find yourself in the lap of your opposite neighbour. The carriages are coupled, jerk goes the engine, and the positions are reversed: you are deposited on your own seat, with your opposite friend's head in contact with your nasal organ...'

Grasscroft Halt, c. 1954. In 1856 the Delph Donkey trains were extended along a new railway from Greenfield to Oldham. Seen here is the stopping-place that was opened in 1912 at the point this line crossed High Grove Road. The Delph-Oldham Clegg Street train will soon be traversing the 1,332 yard long Lydgate Tunnel, a ventilation shaft of which is visible on the skyline. This stretch of railway closed in 1964.

New Delph, *c.* 1910. A heavily-laden cart is manoeuvred out of the yard at Delph station. The load comprises bales of wool for processing in the local factories. In addition to bringing in raw materials, the Delph branch railway was heavily used for the despatch of finished products. These included woollen cloth, much of which went to Liverpool for export. Goods facilities were withdrawn from Delph in 1963.

Delph station. The passenger service to Delph ceased in 1955. The very last train into Delph was the 11.10 p.m. from Clegg Street on Saturday, 30 April. Sixty passengers was the normal load but ten times that number packed into the specially-lengthened train. The platform at Delph was thronged with people, the atmosphere more that of a wake than a funeral.

Denshaw Road, Delph. An enthusiastic user of steam lorries was the calico-printing works at Denshaw. M 1204 was a product of the Foden company of Cheshire. Seen against a backdrop of Eagle Mill, the vehicle is working on what was its usual route at the time, from the yard at Delph station to the printworks. Its solid tyres were not kind to road surfaces in 1923 Saddleworth Council were so concerned about the problem that they debated whether to beg the company to fit their lorry with rubber tyres.

Denshaw, c. 1925. Parked outside the Junction Inn is a road-roller and crew. It is owned by the West Riding County Council, which was responsible for maintaining the principal roads in the district. Other roads in Saddleworth were entrusted to the local authority, which operated their own roller for the purpose. In the 1920s this was a six-tonner that had cost the council £453.

High Street, Uppermill, *c.* 1924. The first bus services in Saddleworth were introduced in the 1920s. One of the companies involved was North Western Road Car, which in 1924 gained licenses to operate a circular route from Oldham through Delph and Uppermill. Seen here is a vehicle used on this service – a Daimler with single-deck brush body. In the background is the Old Factory at the bottom of Smithy Lane.

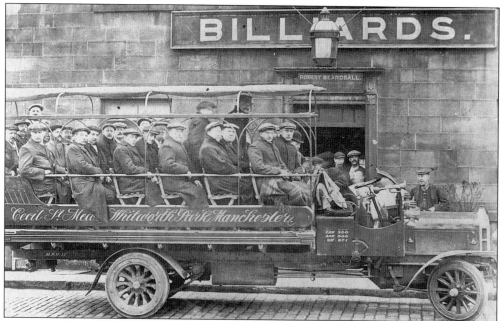

Commercial Hotel, Uppermill, *c.* 1919. Charabancs became popular in Saddleworth just after the First World War. The makeshift appearance of the vehicle seen here, with its spartan seating and rudimentary protection against the elements, would suggest that, like many early 'charas,' it was in actuality a lorry that could be converted to carry passengers when required. One regular operator of such a vehicle at this period was the Delph Co-operative Society, whose lorry would carry groceries during the week and run as the charabanc *Delphina* during the weekend.

Woods Lane, Dobcross, *c.* 1925. These purpose-built charabancs have been hired for a day's outing to Buxton, a bone-rattling thirty miles away on solid tyres. By this date such vehicles were proving serious competitors to the locality's railways. In 1923, for example, a newspaper reported that during the annual 'Wakes' holiday 'there was a perfect stream of charabancs and the railway company has suffered accordingly... 200 went to Blackpool by charabanc and only 170 by train.'

Delph, *c*. 1908. Albert Mallalieu of Rose Hill, Delph, must have been very proud to take delivery of this Argyll motor car. Registered on 19 June 1908, it developed sixteen horsepower and was painted dark green with white lining. Both the vehicle and is chauffeur attest to the wealth of the owner, one of a family of successful industrialists in Delph.

Manchester Road, Greenfield, *c*. 1910. Standing outside the Royal George public house near the crossroads at Ridding is another early car. Motoring in Saddleworth in these pioneering days was not without its hazards, for drivers and pedestrians alike. An early fatality involved a child, who was knocked down in Uppermill in October 1908. Traps were set by the police to discourage the speeding that contributed to such accidents. One of several prosecutions that resulted involved the driver who was estimated to have careered through Scouthead at 25mph.

King Street, Delph, *c.* 1905. This mail cart has drawn-up outside the post office at Delph, its lettering indicating that Edward VII was on the throne. A vehicle of this type operated daily from Oldham. As one was passing through Grasscroft on its way to Delph on 4 February 1911, two men waylaid it, but were repulsed by the driver wielding his whip.

Brownhill, Dobcross, c. 1925. Richly decorated, for an unknown occasion, a horse stands outside the Saddleworth Urban District Council depot at Saddleworth Viaduct. The horse could have been Smiler. On 1 October 1928 the council discussed the fate of their dray horse which had become too old and slow for its work. With a sadness that comes through the minutes which record the occasion, it was resolved that Smiler would have to be put down

Chew Valley Road, Greenfield, c. 1930. A milk float calls at houses opposite the 'Wellington Inn'. The purity of Saddleworth's milk could not always be guaranteed. In November 1909, for example, one customer had complained to the local Medical Officer of Health that 'the milk supplied to him contained large numbers of lice and hair from a human being.'

Airliner crash, Greenfield, 19 August 1949. Failure to make a course correction, together with poor visibility in low cloud, led to a British European Airways Dakota crashing at Wimberry Rocks. Of the twenty-nine passengers and three crew on this regular flight from Belfast to Manchester, just eight passengers survived. Heightening the sense of tragedy was the fact that had the plane been just a few feet higher it would have cleared the hill, the last before its destination.

Seven
Leisure

Saddleworth Handbell Ringers. One way in which church bell-ringers could practice without using steeple bells was to play handbells. The Saddleworth Handbell Ringers were in existence by the 1880s. They gained several prizes for their skills and are photographed after winning a competition at Belle Vue, Manchester, in 1921.

Rushcart building, Uppermill, *c.* 1890. The rushcart was a ceremonial means of conveying the rushes that used to be spread on the floor of Saddleworth church, for warmth and cleanliness. Once a year, traditionally the second Saturday in August, rushcarts would be drawn to the church from the various hamlets and villages that had sponsored their building. As the photograph suggests, making a rushcart required much skill and effort. In addition to the time consumed in the preliminary search for rushes of various sizes and the tying of these into 'bolts', a team of builders needed a minimum of eight hours to complete the task.

Wade Lock, Uppermill, *c.* 1880. A contemporary eulogised the Saddleworth rushcart: 'A more graceful or beautiful structure does not exist than a well-built rushcart, perfectly geometrical in all its faces, no part harsh or angular and all converging into a line of beauty'.

114

The Square, Uppermill, *c.* 1905. Demonstrated here is the method by which a rushcart was drawn using ropes and stangs. The rider sits astride the top of the structure, among the traditional branches of oak and ash. Maintaining balance atop a rushcart could be difficult, especially after over-indulgence in the ale that would flow freely at 'rush-bearing' time. In 1892 one rider toppled to his death in Delph.

Whit Friday, Greenfield, *c.* 1910. After around 1850 the various churches and chapels in Saddleworth began to celebrate Whitsuntide on the same day, the Friday before Trinity Sunday. Thereafter, Whit Friday became perhaps the brightest highlight in the Saddleworth calender. The day would begin with processions between Sunday schools and their respective places of worship. Here we see one such procession moving along Chew Valley Road with the Greenfield Wesleyan Chapel as backcloth.

Saddleworth church, Whit Friday, *c.* 1900. Morning service over, the combined congregations of St Chad's and Kiln Green churches form into the procession that the band, visible in the background, will accompany to Uppermill village. Hymn-singing in The Square and an afternoon of games for the children lie ahead.

Uppermill, Whit Friday, 1910. The culmination of the morning processions would be communal singing. One of the venues for this was Uppermill Square, viewed here from the steps of the Wesleyan Chapel. For a long period the various denominations conducted this part of the day's activities separately but by the date of the photograph the concept of the 'united sing' had finally been accepted.

Dobcross, 1914. The umbrellas raised over the singers in The Square are a reminder that Whit Friday celebrations were ever hostage to the elements. A local newspaper recorded of 1914 that 'because of the rain the Whit processions were a complete failure from the spectacular point of view and one could not but feel sorry for the children trudging along the streets wet to the skin'.

Dobcross, June 1942. A general holiday was called in Saddleworth to celebrate the coronation of Edward VII. One centre of festivities was the Square at Dobcross. Overlooking the Ramsden memorial here is The Swan, an inn built in the mid-eighteenth century and called The King's Head until 1859. In the 1830s it alternated with the Commercial Inn at Uppermill as the venue for magistrates' courts, its cellars being adapted for the temporary holding of prisoners.

Coronation Day, Greenfield, 22 June 1911. Approaching Road End is a celebratory procession that had started from the Royal George Mills. Included were a number of tableaux. The chief of these comprised a miniature King George V and Queen, riding in a coach decorated with satin.

Coronation bonfire, Delph, 1937. The statistics of this were impressive: thirty men, three horses and two motor vehicles took seven weeks to bring the material to the site at Delph Hill; the structure was 40ft in height and weighed 215 tons; 150 gallons of oil, four barrels of tar, one ton of rags and one ton of paper were needed to set the blaze.

Delph Co-operative Society Jubilee, July 1909. The officials gathered on Swan Meadow had much to be proud of. By this date the Delph Co-op had 750 members, ran a savings bank and a library, was actively involved in woollen manufacturing, had recently opened a new store in the village, and had even formed its own choir; good profits and dividends were declared continually. All had not always been so well with the society, however: in 1883 the secretary eloped with a woollen weaver from the village, taking most of his employer's monies with him.

Woods Lane, Dobcross, c. 1935. These vehicles have been decorated for anniversary celebrations of the Dobcross 'co-op'. They are in the vicinity of the grocery store established in 1868 by the rival Uppermill Co-operative Society. The latter had a strong presence at Dobcross; as early as 1866 it had sixty-six members there. Competition was eventually ended by merger of the two societies.

Co-operative Society store, The Square, Dobcross, c. 1935. Until the mid-twentieth century the various co-ops in Saddleworth ran a large number of shops, often several in each village. The main store of the Dobcross Society was one of this multitude. In the window are displayed some of the relatively cheap goods of reliable quality that were associated with the co-operative movement and which contributed to its popularity in the district. This branch closed in 1981.

Grotton Lido, c. 1935. This open-air swimming pool had a brief, but popular, existence between the First and Second World Wars. Apart from a pool, 180ft long that was heated to 75 degrees Fahrenheit, its facilities included a water chute and high diving board. There was also a dance floor and a bandstand, on which the White Star Dance Band would play on Tuesday and Saturday evenings. Sheltered housing, called Lido House now occupies this site, adjacent to Oldham Road.

Henry Taylor, c. 1922. When he retired from competitive swimming in 1926, Henry Taylor had won 35 trophies and 300 medals. Several of the medals were gained at Olympic level, including two gold in the 1908 games in London. Another distinction was his setting in 1914 of a record time for swimming across Morecambe Bay. This legendary, Oldham-born sportsman was the licensee of the Nudger Inn in Dobcross between 1922 and 1924. This photograph was taken at the nearby Platt Lane dam where he used to practice. Often short of money, Mr Taylor would sometimes raffle or sell his trophies over the bar at the Nudger.

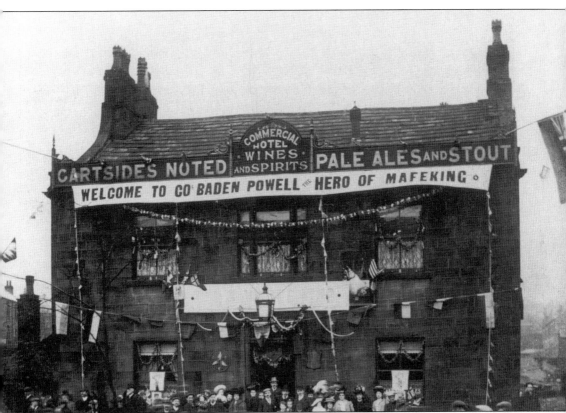

Commercial Hotel, Uppermill, November 1908. Made into one of the most famous men of his time by his dogged defence of Mafeking during the Boer War in 1900, Robert Baden-Powell received an enthusiastic welcome when he visited Uppermill to open a new drill-hall on High Street. As founder of the Boy Scout movement it was fitting that he also inspected Saddleworth scouts, who paraded in The Square opposite this appropriately decorated public house.

White Hart, Lydgate, *c.* 1948. Tap-room regulars await the coach that the landlord, Herbert Walton, has arranged to take them on a day's outing to York. Scrupulous observance of the rule that they should not drink until Wade Lock had been reached was no guarantee against drunkenness, as this location is at Uppermill, only two miles away. Second from the right, on the back row is Ken Bradbury. Every Friday, between the ages of around twelve and seventy, he would wind up the clock at St Anne's church opposite the pub.

Captain Bagnall's Garden Party, August 1909. The upper strata of Saddleworth society flocked to this large event which was held in the grounds of Hawthorpe, a late Victorian detached house on the outskirts of Uppermill. Behind the captain and a group of his guests are Well Meadow – subsequently built over – and the slanting line of Church Road.

Greenfield, c. 1890. The free access to Pots and Pans Hill now taken for granted was gained only after a struggle and the individuals in this photograph would have done well to be vigilant. In 1870, for example, a visiting surgeon and his magistrate friend were each fined for trespassing on Pots and Pans. It took determined effort by the local authority during the 1890s in upholding moorland rights of way before walkers could safely ignore over-zealous landowners and their gamekeepers.

Carte de Visite, c. 1875. This was a product of one of the several photographers' studios that existed in Saddleworth in the late nineteenth century. These pocket-size cards cost around 3s 6d per dozen. At this early stage of photography long exposures were required; in 1872 one studio in Uppermill assured prospective customers that 'children are taken in three seconds.'

This advertisement of around 1870 recalls the most prolific of the Saddleworth portrait photographers. Mr Wilkinson's success owed much to sheer entrepreneurial flair. An example of this was the idea he conceived in 1883 of using the wild, moorland location of Standedge Rocks near Diggle as a setting for portraits of groups. How successful this venture was is not recorded, but as an inducement he promised to give a free copy of the customers' photograph to the organizer of any group who took up the offer.

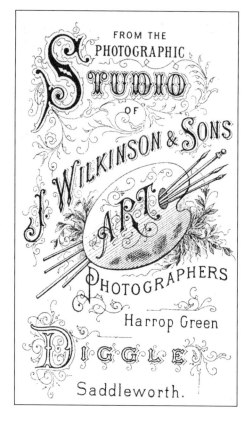

FROM THE
PHOTOGRAPHIC
STUDIO
OF
J. WILKINSON & SONS
ART
PHOTOGRAPHERS
Harrop Green
DIGGLE
Saddleworth.

Midnight Ramblers, *c.* 1910. The recently excavated Roman camp at Castleshaw is the gathering place for these celebrants of the summer solstice. Walking was becoming a popular pastime in Saddleworth at this date; as early as 1893 a footpaths society had been formed to preserve and foster enjoyment of its large network of rights of way.

Cross Keys, Uppermill, *c.* 1930. A visitor to the district in 1849 remarked: 'the weavers of Saddleworth are, like Nimrod, mighty hunters; every third or fourth man keeps his beagle or his brace of beagles'. The group photographed is continuing this strong tradition. The building on the left was converted from house to inn in around 1760. Known for a period as 'Gravemakers', it was built alongside the packhorse track from Standedge to Mottram.